AMAZING STRUCTURES
BRIDGES

by Rebecca Pettiford

pogo

Ideas for Parents and Teachers

Pogo Books let children practice reading informational text while introducing them to nonfiction features such as headings, labels, sidebars, maps, and diagrams, as well as a table of contents, glossary, and index.

Carefully leveled text with a strong photo match offers early fluent readers the support they need to succeed.

Before Reading

- "Walk" through the book and point out the various nonfiction features. Ask the student what purpose each feature serves.
- Look at the glossary together. Read and discuss the words.

Read the Book

- Have the child read the book independently.
- Invite him or her to list questions that arise from reading.

After Reading

- Discuss the child's questions. Talk about how he or she might find answers to those questions.
- Prompt the child to think more. Ask: Have you ever been on an especially memorable bridge? What was it like?

Pogo Books are published by Jump!
5357 Penn Avenue South
Minneapolis, MN 55419
www.jumplibrary.com

Library of Congress Cataloging-in-Publication Data

Pettiford, Rebecca, author.
 Bridges / by Rebecca Pettiford.
  pages cm. – (Amazing structures)
 Audience: Ages 7-9.
 Includes bibliographical references and index.
 ISBN 978-1-62031-211-7 (hardcover: alk. paper) –
 ISBN 978-1-62496-298-1 (ebook)
 1. Bridges–Juvenile literature. I. Title.
 TG148.P48 2016
 624.2–dc23
                                    2014042533

Series Editor: Jenny Fretland VanVoorst
Series Designer: Anna Peterson
Photo Researcher: Anna Peterson

Photo Credits: All photos by Shutterstock except: Alamy, 12-13; Dreamstime, 6-7, 10; Getty 4, 18.

Printed in the United States of America at Corporate Graphics in North Mankato, Minnesota.

TABLE OF CONTENTS

CHAPTER 1
Why Do We Use Bridges? 4

CHAPTER 2
Types of Bridges 10

CHAPTER 3
Building Bridges 18

ACTIVITIES & TOOLS
Try This! 22
Glossary 23
Index 24
To Learn More 24

CHAPTER 1

WHY DO WE USE BRIDGES?

Did you ever see a tree lying across a stream? Did you walk on it to get to the other side?

Long ago, trees that fell across streams may have given people the idea for building bridges.

Bridges make our lives easier.
They help us cross rivers,
roads, and valleys.
Without them, we would
have to walk farther.

Early bridges were made
of stone, wood, and rope.
Today, builders also use
steel and **concrete**.

DID YOU KNOW?

Did you know that animals use bridges too? Wildlife crossings are bridges built to help animals cross busy roads. In doing so, they prevent car accidents. They save the lives of people and animals.

Bridges have to be strong to handle both the weight of traffic and the bridge itself. They have to stand up to strong winds and changing weather.

There are several types of bridges. Let's look at a few.

CHAPTER 2

TYPES OF BRIDGES

A **beam bridge** has a simple shape. It uses a firm beam and a **pier** at each end.

beam

pier

If the piers are far apart, the beam will not be as strong. Most beams are made of steel or concrete.

arch

An **arch bridge** is one of the oldest bridge designs. It has been used for more than 3,000 years.

Its strength comes from its curved shape. The arch presses down from the top. The ground resists with the same force.

DID YOU KNOW?

Most bridges are fixed. They don't have any moving parts. But **lift bridges** have a movable roadway. The road can be raised to allow ships to pass underneath.

tower

cables

On a **suspension bridge** the road hangs from **cables**. The cables hang between two or more towers.

The towers bear most of the weight. Supporting cables are fixed to solid rock or large concrete blocks called **anchorages**.

This bridge often has a **truss** under the road. It looks like a pattern of short triangles. It keeps the bridge strong and steady in the wind.

TAKE A LOOK!

Many parts work together to make a bridge safe.

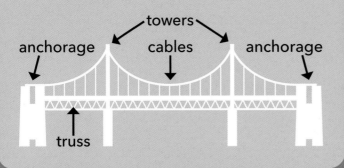

towers

anchorage   cables   anchorage

truss

truss

CHAPTER 3

BUILDING BRIDGES

Bridge engineers plan and build new bridges. They make sure a bridge can support all the weight it must carry.

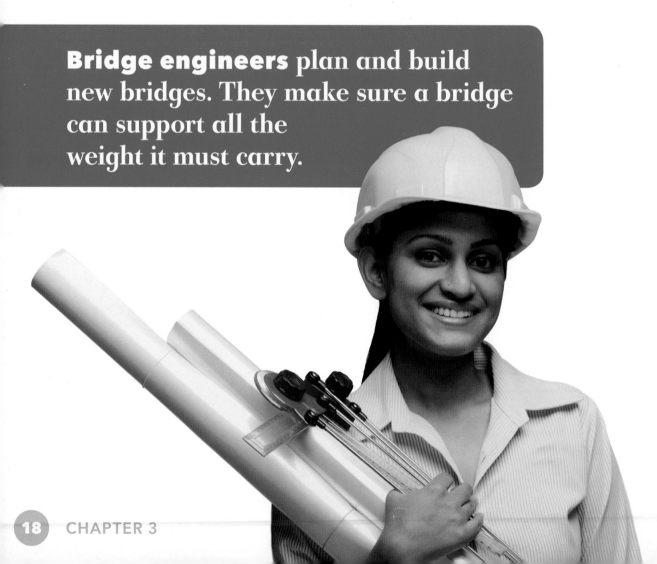

They make sure it is steady in strong wind and bad weather. They also fix older bridges so they are safe to use.

Engineers want to make bridges that can handle more traffic and heavier loads. To do this, they will need to find new ways to make bridges stronger. Do you think they can do it?

ACTIVITIES & TOOLS

BUILD A BEAM BRIDGE

Let's build a beam bridge and discover how the distance between supports affects the bridge's strength. You will need:

- two plastic cups
- one 8.5 × 3 inch (22 × 8 centimeter) strip of construction paper
- 25 or more pennies
- tape

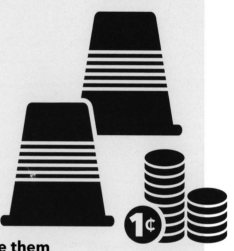

❶ Place two cups upside down and space them about two inches (5 cm) apart.

❷ Place the paper strip on top of the two cups. Tape the strip to the cups.

❸ Once your paper strip is in place, add one penny on top of the strip. Keep adding pennies. How many pennies did your bridge hold before it collapsed?

❹ Now, move the cups farther apart. Do the experiment again. Is this second bridge weaker or stronger than the first? Why?

GLOSSARY

anchorages: Solid rock or large concrete blocks; a bridge's supporting cables are fixed to anchorages.

arch bridge: A bridge in which the main supporting structures are arches.

beam bridge: A simple bridge structure that uses a firm beam and a supporting pier at each end.

bridge engineers: People who help plan and build bridges.

cables: A strong, thick rope made of twisted wires.

concrete: A mix of broken stone or gravel, sand, cement, and water, that hardens after it is spread or poured.

lift bridge: A bridge that raises its roadway in order to allow water traffic to pass beneath.

pier: A solid structural support.

truss: A metal framework that supports a bridge.

steel: A metal made from iron and carbon.

suspension bridge: A bridge that hangs from cables which are supported by towers; its support cables are fixed to solid rock or anchorages.

INDEX

anchorages 15

arch bridge 12-13

beam bridge 10, 11

beams 10, 11

cables 15

concrete 7, 11, 15

engineers 18

lift bridge 13

piers 10, 11

rope 7

steel 7, 11

stone 7

suspension bridge 14-15, 16-17

towers 15

traffic 8, 21

trees 4, 5

truss 16

weather 8, 19

wildlife crossings 7

wind 8, 16, 19

TO LEARN MORE

Learning more is as easy as 1, 2, 3.

1) Go to www.factsurfer.com

2) Enter "bridges" into the search box.

3) Click the "Surf" to see a list of websites.

With factsurfer, finding more information is just a click away.